GRACE to LEAD

THE MAN'S DIVINE ROLE IN THE FAMILY

DR. WUNMI LAWAL

"*Grace to Lead: The Man's Divine Role in the Family* by Dr. Lawal serves as an accessible introduction to its subject, offering clarity in a time of gender confusion. It provides a clear framework for beginners, using biblical verses to engage readers and guide them through ten chapters. The book includes relevant scripture, prayers, and suggestions for further reading, making it ideal for slow readers or those easily distracted. It effectively helps fathers visualize their leadership role in their families and encourages raising sons to become strong, godly men."

—Dr. Patrick Akinbola

"*Grace to Lead: The Man's Divine Role in the Family* is an excellent resource for men who are seeking to understand their purpose in life. It discusses leadership in a way that expands personal growth and spiritual leadership. The book can be used by prayer accountability partners or a larger study group. It inspires readers to step into their full potential as God's chosen gatekeepers. Finally, while the book is primarily aimed at men, it is also a valuable read for anyone interested in exploring qualities of leadership, responsibility, and spiritual maturity in relationships."

—Ngozi Onunaku Lawal

"*Grace to Lead: The Man's Divine Role in the Family* concisely explains the honor bestowed on man as the head of the family. This position comes with a significant responsibility, but man is biologically equipped with the physical strength to administer this amazing role. This book is full of rich nuggets that remind man of who he is, his true position in the family as the gate keeper who safeguards, and controls what and who enters the home."

—Rev. Catherine Idigo, RN, MSN, MBA

PRESENTED TO

_____

FROM

_____

DATED

_____

Copyright © 2020, 2025 Dr. Omowunmi A. Lawal.

All rights reserved. No part of this book may be reproduced, stored, or transmitted by any means—whether auditory, graphic, mechanical, or electronic—without written permission of both publisher and author, except in the case of brief excerpts used in critical articles and reviews. Unauthorized reproduction of any part of this work is illegal and is punishable by law.

Unless otherwise indicated, scripture quotations are taken from The New King James Version of the Holy Bible.

ISBN: 979-8-89419-613-8 (sc)
ISBN: 979-8-89419-614-5 (hc)
ISBN: 979-8-89419-615-2 (e)

Because of the dynamic nature of the Internet, any web addresses or links contained in this book may have changed since publication and may no longer be valid. The views expressed in this work are solely those of the author and do not necessarily reflect the views of the publisher, and the publisher hereby disclaims any responsibility for them.

Further enquiries must be directed to:
Dr. Wunmi Abiodun Lawal
+1(240 599-8026. +1 (732) 822-5029
Email: wumylaw@gmail.com, goalawal@gmail.com.

One Galleria Blvd., Suite 1900, Metairie, LA 70001
(504) 702-6708

CONTENTS

Introduction vii

Acknowledgments xi

ONE: Acknowledge God's Bestowed Honor 1

TWO: Be Prepared to Play the role 7

THREE: Love and honor your wife 11

FOUR: Be Your Family Royal Priesthood 15

FIVE: Be Your Family Provider 19

SIX: Be Your Family Guard Rail 22

SEVEN: Be a Firm leader in Your Home 25

EIGHT: Give Your Children What Matters Most 28

NINE: Align with God's Will, Plan, and Purpose 34

TEN: Man: A Pillar of Purpose in Church,
Community, and the World 38

ELEVEN: The ABCs of Salvation 42

INTRODUCTION

When God created the first human being, he had an intentioned, deliberate desire to make the first being a man. In his infinite wisdom and understanding, he placed Adam in the precious Garden of Eden, to tend, cultivate and dominate the land.

The reason for God's action is not a happenstance, it was a willful action, and he alone knew the plan and purpose for why he did that.

It may appear as a paradox, that the same God that created Adam to have dominion on the Garden, is the same God that fashioned Eve out of him, to assist him, be his helpmate, and ensure the man succeeds in everything he is commanded to do.

This book seeks to ignite the appreciation of every man, and to encourage him to see how God has honored him, and how much responsibility he has placed upon him to take care of other human lives bestowed unto him, those of his wife and children.

It is to his honor, and the glory of God, that man is divinely, and unilaterally chosen, honored beyond his limited power, his righteousness, or faithfulness to God. But bestowed upon him, out of God's deliberate, though inexplicable, unfathomable, wisdom and love, the magnificence of such an honorable position.

This title, gatekeeper, gives man the overall power and authority to give access to what he approves or disapproves what he considers to be inappropriate for his family. This same position is an exclusive responsibility which he can operate on his own without the consent of, or approval of the woman, his wife who is to be his help meet.

The man, with this bestowed title, could misuse and abuse his position as the gatekeeper of his family, without realizing the implications of his actions. If he is unguarded, undisciplined, lacks discernment and unwise and not meticulous in his decisions, he may jeopardize the safety, trust, joy, and wellness of his family and household, which the Lord has confidently, respectably, and honorably entrusted to him, despite his probable and known vulnerability, frailty, and weakness.

As the head of the family, the man, who is the father whose children bear his name as their last name, and stays with the male children forever, also have his wife bear his name until they are divorced, is given so much latitude and free reign to make and take decisions on behalf of his wife, the children and the entire family at large.

The man, by God's grace has the enablement, he is empowered to nurture, train, provide, protect, preserve, and take calculated risks on behalf of his family. As the appointed head of the household, he is ordained according to God's ordinances and principles to care, love, work and preserve the affairs of his family. He is regarded by God as the gatekeeper of his family; the one who has the baton of authority and power to ameliorate or escalate situation according to his wisdom and understanding and settles issues and concerns affecting his family and his household. The one in whose hands the lives of many unique human lives are placed. Though, this may prove to be a herculean task, but it is indeed a great and majestic honor to bestow on any individual, and God in his Omniscient power and integrity placed this tribute on the shoulder of man.

This concept called Grace to Lead, is an inexplicable, unfathomable wisdom of God bestowed on man. The man's due diligence is to receive it, accept it, be grateful for the underserved abundant gift, and continue to work in alignment with the Lord's will, plan, and purpose for his life. If he will adhere to this his way will surely be prosperous and he would actualize and manifest good success with unparallelled peace.

ACKNOWLEDGMENTS

How can any man claim to have, or own anything without acknowledging the one who creates him in the first instance? Therefore, there could never have been me without the Creator of heaven and earth. I consider myself a branch in the vine of Christ, my savior, and my Master.

If it had not been for his grace and favor, I am sure this book and previous ones could not have been birth. I am in awe of his infinite, amazing grace upon my life.

I do not know where I would have been without this precious, magnificent God. He is a faithful, consistent, and honorable God. He has blessed me with his words, his spirit of courage and inexplicable strength to do the humble things I am empowered to do; and the gift of writing is one of them. Hence, my life honors him, I avow him as God over everything that I am, all I own, and all I will ever become. Therefore, I return all praise, adoration, honor, and glory to him. He alone deserves my gratitude from now till eternity.

The book is dedicated to my son, grandsons, and all loving, caring, God-fearing fathers, husbands, and men in the land, and in the vineyard of God's kingdom. May they continue to honor the glory God has wisely and graciously bestowed unto them.

CHAPTER ONE

Acknowledge God's Bestowed Honor

> *In the beginning was the Word, and the Word was with God, and the Word was God. He was in the beginning with God. All things were made through him, and without him was not anything made that was made. In him was life, and the life was the light of men. The light shines in the darkness, and the darkness has not overcome it. John 1:1-51*

Adam, the first man God created in his own image and likeness, from the dirt of the earth, received the breath of life from God, and he became a living being. He was deliberately, divinely, and graciously placed into the resplendent and majestic place, called the Garden of Eden.

This was a glamorous place, loaded and equipped with all Adam will ever need to live a fulfilled life that will make him thrive and flourish. Nonetheless, Adam sowed a seed of willful disobedience. But, ashamedly and disastrously, Adam overplayed his hand and reaped a whirlwind. (Genesis 1:26-30).

It is unsearchable the wisdom of God; and from the onset, God deliberately and determinedly chose to create man as the first human entity. This is not because man has done anything to deserve it, it is not because he is superior to the woman, or because of his holiness or righteousness, But for Gods divine, inexplicable knowledge and wisdom, he bestowed this honor on a man, and he made him the commander-in-chief of the Garden of Eden. He gave Adam authority and control over everything he created. Adam had no part in the creation of anything that he had, except to dominate and control. In one sense, Adam indeed, had everything cut out for him.

Nonetheless, it is inexplicable how any person with such an easy start will want anything more. But the Bible was explicit about the deliberate act of willful disobedience perpetrated by Adam through the manipulation of the devil and the conviction of his helpmate, Adam hurt God, he disappointed God, God could have obliterated him and he could have been worse, but God was merciful to him. But God allowed him to keep his authority, dominate, and control, retain his honor.

As it was with Adam, so it is with the modern husband today. If he is in Christ, he is called the chosen generation, a royal priesthood, a holy nation, and says he has taken you from darkness into his marvelous light (1 Peter 2:9). Because of the various blessings bestowed on him, he ought to show allegiance, loyalty, and honor God for freely giving these benefits. This is one of the most honorable ways, the Lord has blessed a man, and he ought to acknowledge this as a privilege, accept it as an honor and appreciate it because you have not worked or contributed to it.

Nonetheless, Despite Adams belligerence and disrespect for God's specific instruction, God forgave him. Although, he went away with tough and severe sanctions. Adam now must labor where he once had a free control, easy access to God, free resource of food and vegetation, secured, fortified, resplendent habitation, calmness and peace of body, soul, and spirit.

The same situation is on today. Every man, every husband, every head of household is mandated to have dominion over everything God created; and when he aligns his will with God, he will discover that the spirit of God will support him in all his endeavors. Therefore, the head of the household ought to appreciate God's immense favor and honor on him.

This inexplicable generous and compassionate spirit of God, is what today's man must acknowledge, acclaim, and appreciate. God, in his pure and just judgement could have obliterated Adam for his heinous crime and chose to create another human being. But knows the heart of man, that is deceitful and desperately wicked (Jeremiah 17:9). He is the only one who knows and understands him; and in his infinite and infallible knowledge and unfathomable wise judgment, he chose to forgive Adam.

At this stage, it is imperative that man, as an offshoot of his obstinate ancestor, must appreciate the position God has bestowed on him honorably, and align his will, desires, plan, and purpose to that which God had designed for him.

Nonetheless, why would God choose the man as the gatekeeper of the home? Fortunately, no created being of God has the infinite knowledge or wisdom of God. The Bible indicates that long before the first human being was formed, God already intentioned to create man first, he said this in Genesis 1:26, and he knew the roles and the responsibilities he wants to lay on his shoulders. Therefore, no one can question God, who created everything and everyone, whom he should choose to be the gatekeeper of the home.

What then does the gatekeeper do? The dictionary defines a gatekeeper, as the individual that gives access or blocks access to a place. In a spiritual context, a gatekeeper is an individual, mandated to represent God on earth, taking care of his children, devoted to his wife, nurturing, teaching, providing, and leading his children in the way and admonition of the Lord. He is supposed to be an example of virtue and good behavior to his children, exemplary role model to his community, and others in his circle of influence. He has the power and wherewithal to protect, shield, provide, and stand as a buffer against his family's infiltrator (Ephesians 5:23) (1 Corinthians 11:3).

The bible alludes to Jesus, the only Begotten Son, as the true shepherd and the gatekeeper by whom the children of God will come into God's kingdom. This definition presupposes that a gatekeeper is a safety guard of his home. He is regarded as the first and last stop. He is mandated to love his family, provide for them, and go the extra distance for them in times of trouble and trial. He is expected to replicate what Jesus Christ was to his disciples while he was alive.

Christ is referred to as always going about healing the sick people, reviving the weak and raising the dead, while delivering those that are possessed and tormented by demons and enemies (Acts 10:38).

Hence, the man is seen and accepted as the one responsible to take on the dirty job, severe blow, assault, and even death on behalf of his family, if the circumstance calls for it. Aside from providing for the members of his household. He is also expected to be the rock his family stand on and the shoulder they fall on for their needs and desires to be fulfilled, and the one expected to resolve their dire circumstances, troubles, and calamity.

However, the choice of the man chosen as the gatekeeper of the family has nothing to do with his prowess, ability, wisdom, or righteousness. This was a divine providence and the absolute wisdom, knowledge, and desire of the Almighty Father.

It is in the face of man's acceptance, acknowledgment, obedience, and appreciation of what God has done, that will give man innate knowledge, understanding and wisdom, which in turn will subsequently translate into honorable path, prosperous way, and good success for him, just as God advised Joshua (Joshua 1:8).

If man knows what is good for me, He should accept the role, and the responsibility God has placed upon him. In his myopic understanding, an unmarried man, who has always been responsible for himself, may find it odd and stressful to want to add on the responsibility of taking care of a woman, another individual, whom he knows less than 70% about. But this is the opposite to what he thinks.

In God's wise perspective, he thinks that a man, from the time of Adam, needs the help of a woman to assist him achieve the goal and purpose for which God has created him. In the Bible, it states that a man that finds a woman, who will stay with him, help him accomplish his God given purpose, has indeed finds a good thing, and the individual has obtained favor from God (Proverbs 18:22).

At this point, a man who has matured, has been able to find a responsible and equally matured woman, should go ahead and become married. This act is not to be taken lightly, but to be entered into as a covenant of righteousness, holiness and everlasting one, with God as the divine partner.

From the point a man got married to his wife, he no longer remains responsible for himself alone. He is now the head of the household. The household is now him and his wife. He is now a family person, head of the household, and a husband.

This husband and head of household role must be taken seriously. This man must be intentional, prepared, and ready to adapt to this position. As a husband, he has a list of responsibilities that he must carry out.

When you have accepted these roles, you must be ready to seek for help not only from the woman, but that person, who is also now your wife, and your responsibility. You must be ready to ask God for help in all aspects of your endeavor, where you may be lacking in skills, efforts, and strength. God says he is ready to assists you when you seek and call on him for assistance (Matthew 7:7).

When you call on God for help and you have conviction that he will assist, then, he will show you great and mighty things that you do not know, or aware of. This is how deep God is willing to go with you on this new marriage adventure (Jeremiah 33:3).

However, it is essential to know that if you as a man and a husband, is willing to succeed, you must collaborate with God, on the basis of his rules, ordinances, precepts, and commandments. If you follow his dictates, there is a certainty that you will experience prosperity and success in all that you have endeavored to do.

Prayer

Father Lord, I thank you for bestowing me with the honor of the head of the household, I bless you because you counted me worthy of the role of a man; Lord, grant me the wisdom and the grace to uphold and practice this role and its responsibilities with courage and steadfastness, in the name of Jesus, Amen.

References

Genesis 1:1-2:25, Genesis 2:1-25, Psalm 93:1-5, Ecclesiastes 1:4-5, Ezekiel 16:48-49, Matthew 22:37, Mark 10:1, Mark 12:18, Luke 21:1-4, John 1:1-51, Romans 1:26.

CHAPTER TWO

Be Prepared to Play the role

Likewise, husbands, live with your wives in an understanding way, showing honor to the woman as the weaker vessel, since they are heirs with you of the grace of life, so that your prayers may not be hindered. 1 Peter 3:7

The role of a man in a home is not a child's play. In fact, except a man is matured and have the support and grace of God, he may not succeed as a husband, a father, and the head of the household.

The institution of marriage originates from God himself. He fashioned the first wife, Eve, for the first man Adam. When he established this relationship, God did not specifically identify Eve's role as a wife and her husband's help meet. However, this presupposes that Eve's role will be dependent on whatever assistance her husband required from her. This same is applicable to any woman, any wife of a man, a husband.

Nonetheless, Adam's role and responsibilities were designed for him by God. At first, God brought all the animals to him, and Adam named the animals as he had unction and utterance of the spirit. Then the Lord asked Adam to tend to the garden of Eden, and in tending and cultivating the land, Adam also looked after the needs of his wife, Eve.

In the same vein, any man, who is married, is imbued with the same responsibilities to take care of his home, his wife, children, and their needs. The Bible indicates that the failure of a married man, and husband takes its root from the failure to provide for his wife and children. The scripture says "But if any provide not for his own, and especially for those of his house, he hath denied the faith, and is worse than an infidel (1 Timothy 5:8). The Bible is saying a man is a failure and irresponsible, if he failed to take care of the needs of people of his family.

This concept of irresponsibility placed on a married man, for failure to discharge his duties and tasks as a married man, are not seriously accepted in many quarters, by the men folks. Others argued that, in a marriage, the woman, the wife, according to Bible instructions are unequivocally mandated the woman, the wife to be in charge of running the home. But is this what the Bible asserts? No, the Bible does not mandate that women run the home, but to be keeper of home" and a helper to the man, her husband (Titus 2).

Nonetheless, because of deep and inadequate understanding, and wisdom of the Biblical ordinances on marriage, myriads of men have lost on their favors, blessings and prosperity as God has prescribed. Many uphold the thought that a wife is just as responsible for the maintenance and upkeep of the home as her husband. The men who subscribe to this argument maintained that it takes two to run the home successfully both physically and financially. Therefore, it is accepted that a wife has every reason to contribute sufficiently to the upkeep of a home which she shares liberally and equally with her husband. As a result of this perspective, many husbands have sent their wives into sheer stressful labor force, which has failed to provide the needed financial contribution, the husband had earlier envisaged will help the collective income of the family.

Nonetheless, it has been ascertained that in the bid of the home to have a higher collection of income, it has been found that the children in the home, are often found to suffer the impact of their mother long hours of absence from the home, especially when the kids are still in their formative stage of growth.

Husband, your role as the head of the household, father of your children, breadwinner of the family, is for you to live up to the role of the head. The head of a home is the one responsible for ambience and the stabilizing the tranquility of the home, ensuring that the wife, the mother, of the home is adequately provided for, the children of the home are given appropriate educational training, safety, moral ethos, and spiritual guidelines nutritionally fed, and securely protected. These are the core elements of your responsibility.

However, you must know that if you fail to respond and live up to your responsibilities, if you fail to take diligent care of your wife and provide adequately for your children, you may be short-changing yourself. The favor, which the Lord has promised may elude you, the joy which should come naturally will be hindered and short lived, and the peace which should flow easily and unparalleled in your home and in your family will be curtailed and limited.

For you to experience prosperity and unlimited good success, you must work with God, align your desires, will, plan, and purpose with that which God has originally designed for your life and destiny.

Prayer

My Father and my Lord, I thank you for the preparation of a divine, successful, marital relationship. Oh Lord, my God, grant me the divine strength and will to work prosperously with the knowledge and wisdom you have imparted to me. Thank you for making me a caring and providing husband and father for my family, in Jesus' name.

References

Genesis 2:24, 3:28, Proverbs 18:22, 31:1-31, Mark 10:45, Romans 8:28, 1 Corinthians 7:3-5, 11:3, Ephesians 5:1-33, Ephesians 5:22, Colossians 3:18, 1 Timothy 2:11-15, 1 Timothy 3:1-16, 1 Peter 3:3-6, Revelation 22:1-21.

CHAPTER THREE

Love and honor your wife

Likewise, husbands, live with your wives in an understanding way, showing honor to the woman as the weaker vessel, since they are heirs with you of the grace of life, so that your prayers may not be hindered. 1 Peter 3:7

Despite all the instructions given to man. God particularly mandates a man, under the covenant of holy matrimony, a lawfully wedded husband, to love his wife, be kindhearted, and forgives her in case of any infraction, just as Christ in God forgave all repented sinners.

Marriage was the first institution enacted by God; and in his infinite wisdom, a husband is expected to command his wife's respect and honor, he is specifically commanded to love, cherish her, provide, protect, and be ready to sacrifice his life for her, as Christ did for the church.

Being a husband, is a tough order for many men, several men consider the responsibilities a herculean task, too stressful and dreadful for any ordinary man.

As a result of inadequate readiness, preparedness, immaturity, and lack of trust in the Lord, that established the institution to see them through, many failed to adhere and follow through with the laid down ordinances and doctrines of the institution. Subsequently, many derail along the pathway of the marriage journey, and end up in the bottomless valley of pain, anguish, sorrow, and regret.

The first institution God enacted is the institution of marriage. When God brought Eve to Adam, through his supernatural, inexplicable surgery, Adam himself acclaimed that Eve was resplendent and beautiful. He adjudged her the bone of his bones, and flesh of his flesh. Adam substantiated his assertion when he declared that Eve is a woman, because she was brought out of him (Genesis 2:23).

The Bible made us understand that entering the marriage relationship, should be diligently managed. It is not a game for the timid, devious and the undisciplined. It must be seen from the perspective of a life and death issue, hell, and heaven concern. For complex, indescribable reasons, many marriages have landed several couples in the valley of disaster, chaos, and sudden death.

Marriage counselors have theorized the reasons why many husbands in marriages crash and ruin their homes and failed to survive the challenges of the time. It became evident that vices that many considered harmless have turned around to put many marriages into jeopardy.

Many husbands may ruin their marriages and dishonor their wives, and work in tandem against the laid down principles of what a man must be to his wife. The Bible is replete with stories of husbands that love their wives, but also honor and cherish them.

We learned that from the book of Job, the main hero was a caring man called Job. He was an upright, loving, and devoted father, a man God considered honorable and righteous. However he had a terrible calamity brought upon him by Satan; and when his wife advised him to curse God. We did not hear or read of Job disparaging his wife, he still showed her love and considered her advice as unrighteous and unreasonable, but he did not insult or abuse his wife in any form or shape (Ephesians 5, Colossians 3, Matt.19:6).

There are several sins that man could commit that will stand treacherous before God. But there are seven heinous and deadly sins, that the Lord abhors and considered abominable to him. These sins are regarded to cause more harm and damage than could be accounted for. These known abominable concerns are pride, greed, lust, envy, gluttony, wrath, and sloth (Proverbs 6:16-19).

Lust is one of the deadliest sins alluded to in the Bible. This abominable act involved desiring what is not meant for one, chasing after, and craving for others material and non-material things. Women are the most common tools of lust. Lust is known to be a yearning, egregious activity that has brought unimaginable shame, loss, calamity, and even premature death to many men and women. Lust comes in various forms and shades. It could be lust for power, money, position, or for a man or woman. But whichever shape it comes, it is always deadly, ending in troubles, woes, and calamity.

The remaining abominable sins, which comprise anger, Greed, wrath, sloth, pride, and envy, are not any less egregious and destructive. The issue with pride is what landed Satan in hell. He wanted to covet the sovereignty and supreme position of God, just because he had the privilege to minister in the presence of the Almighty God. His insane pride made him caused war in heaven, and he succeeded in taking away one-third of the angels in heaven.

The implications of these abominable acts are too alarming for any discerning and godly husband to dabble into or embrace.

Anger and wrath are other abominable concerns that can set a man ablaze, an angry husband is regarded as a fool, and he may cause mayhem, emotional, and psychological stress and destruction for himself, wife, and his family. Jealousy and envy are illicit twins-sisters sin that has sent many husbands, with unmanageable self-control, to prison and some to premature death.

Nonetheless, the Bible denotes the attendant benefits and blessings accrued to a husband, who demonstrates gentleness, love, the spirit of kindness and generosity with his wife. It declares that such man will be a man of valor, he will have the respect and honor of his peers and friends. His wife will honor and call him Lord, as Sarah did with Abraham (1 Peter 3:6).

Prayer

Heavenly father, I thank you for your unconditional love for me that surpasses all human understanding. Lord, grant the willing heart and generous spirit that will extend your deep, caring love, comfort, and kindness as a husband to my wife, that I may enjoy your favor, blessing, and the respect of my wife, children, and neighbors, in Jesus' name.

References

Genesis 2:24, Proverbs 5:18-18, 12:4, Proverbs 18:22, Matthew 19:4-6, 1 Corinthians 13:4-8, Ephesians 5:23,25, 28,33, Colossians 3:14,19, 1 Peter 3:7.

CHAPTER FOUR

Be Your Family Royal Priesthood

> *For you are a chosen race, a royal priesthood, a holy nation, a people for his own possession, that you may proclaim the excellencies of him who called you out of darkness into his marvelous light. Once you were not a people, but now you are God's people; once you had not received mercy, but now you have received mercy. 1 Peter 2:9-10*

The Bible gave the gory detail of the first murder recorded in the history of humanity. We are despondent by the calamity that befell the first created family. When Cain, the older son of Adam, in cold blood killed his own brother out of his uncontrolled jealousy, envy and anger.

Since this horrific event, it became clear that the man, the husband, and the father, who is placed in charge of his family as the head of the household, had failed woefully to discharge the aspect of being his family spiritual head.

Among the gifts God endowed man, is the gift of his ability to communicate with him through prayer. A husband and father of the household is the man God has handed over his family spiritual petition and needs. We see that God first created Adam, gave me the mantle of authority to tend, cultivate and dominate all he has created, including the animals. Adam was at this, not even noticing that anything was amiss. It was God in Omniscience that knew that something was amiss in Adam's life. He went ahead, without consulting Adam, and brought Eve out of him to complement him and be his helpmeet.

In the context of the secular world, the chief executor officer is the man at the helms of affairs in his organization. He calls all the shots, he knew what the company lacks and needs, he knew whom he should be fired, and what are the strengths, the weakness, the opportunities, and the threats that face his company. A subordinate will not call for the management meeting, a subordinate will not apply for a bank loan behind the back of the chief executive officer of the company. It is not heard of where the subordinate dissolves a corporation established by the chief executive personnel in the company.

However, we observed this gap in the case of Adam, the chosen head of the family, a husband, and a father. The role God gave him, included being the gatekeeper of his family. As the spiritual needs, he is mandated to petition God on behalf of his family, issues concerning his children, the sanity and peace of his relationship with his wife, and the plan and purpose that God have for his family.

Nonetheless, in the case of the family, it was evident that Adam may have not been seeking the face of God on a constant and regular basis. The outcome of his two sons, was an indication that not enough prayers are said, and he did not spend ample time in the war room wrestling with God for answers to his family issues.

At this moment, it is appropriate to mention that many husbands and fathers have not taken seriously the spiritual work that is required of them, therefore they do not know the impending danger, the lurking temptation at the corner, the scheme and manipulation of enemies and Satan waiting to act. Therefore, they fail to anticipate the implications of their lack of their prayerlessness, not communing with God on behalf of their family.

Husbands and Fathers have moral obligation and mandate to seek the face of God on behalf of their family, they are to bring unnatural issues, problem with their prodigal child, obstinate and quarrelsome and a lazy wife, and other protracted thorny concerns that have defied normal answer.

The spiritual head of the house is honored to bring the ordinances and principles of God to the members of his household, and to lead them in the proper path as laid down in God's manual. In Joshua 1:8, made it known to Joshua that he must teach his children the word of God, teaching them the laws, the principles and ordinances of God, and when they follow and obey these, God says they will experience prosperity and will have good success.

Favored man of God, husband of Daughter of Zion, and father of children of the kingdom, the Lord is asking you to move closer to him. He wants you to present your home, the challenges of your home, the situation and conditions affecting your children, your career, and the purpose of God for your family.

Failure to take this role seriously may lead to untold woes and calamity, as was recorded in the situation of Priest Eli, where he was care-free with the spiritual stance of his home, and the children became wayward and aggressive to the things of God, and ended up losing their lives, out of foolish frivolities, lack of honor and reverence for God. Their father's prayer would have set their hearts and souls aright, and would not have perished as they did, if Eli the priest father had fulfilled his responsibility as the spiritual and the priest of his household.

There are blessings that will address your closeness and walking with God; if you follow the directions and obey his commandments. You will experience unparallel peace and joy in the family, and you will see the hand of God in the lives of your children, and your honor and respect shall be multiplied with the wife God has favored you with, and she will do you good, just as the Lord has declared. In Isaiah 8:18, the word of God also declared that the children he has given you shall be for signs and wonders. They will be taught of the Lord, and their peace shall be great, they shall be established in righteousness, they will be far removed from oppression, and whoever gathered together to hurt or harm them shall fall for their sake because no weapon fashioned against them will be established and every word of curses or incantations will remain condemned (Isaiah 54:13-17) These and many more are the attendant benefits that will accrue to any man, who takes the mantle of the spiritual leadership of his home and family. He will receive substantial, unimaginable blessings from the Lord without sorrow added to it.

Prayer

Oh Lord my Father, as you have favored and blessed me with a gracious help meet, Father, quicken my inner man that I may have the will, strength, and grace to stand in the gap for my family as their royal priesthood, in the name of Jesus. Amen.

References

Genesis 2:18-24, Genesis 3:1-24, Psalm 139:1-24, Proverbs 31:1-31, Acts 20:28, 1 Corinthians 11:3, Ephesians 5:1-33, Colossians 3:19, 1 Timothy 5:8, Titus 2:1-15, Hebrews 10:25.

CHAPTER FIVE

Be Your Family Provider

> *But if anyone does not provide for his relatives, and especially for members of his household, he has denied the faith and is worse than an unbeliever. 1 Timothy 5:8*

The provision of the home and the family by a husband and a father is a sacrosanct duty mandated by God for a married man and a head of the household. It is not an option for a husband of the house to elect to provide for his wife, or not. It is a commandment. However, if he fails to comply with this mandate, the Bible castigates him, labelled, and compared him to an unbeliever, who knows nothing about God's principles or ordinances.

It is easy to understand where a husband comes from, when he is reluctant to provide for his family, especially his wife. Several husbands theorized that their wives had a means of subsistence long before they were married. Therefore, there is nothing wrong if she continues to provide for her needs, while he takes care of things which concern both of them, such as the mortgage of the house, the maintenance of the car, and other non-personal essentials.

This mindset in some husbands is a sign of lack of complete understanding of their role as the head of the household, and an unbrokenness of the heart and soul, and this is an egregious behavior before the Lord. On the other hand, many husbands forget that the Bible says that the head of every man is Christ, the head of a wife is her husband, and the head of Christ is God1 Corinthians 11:13. This statement presupposes that Christ as the head of the church provides for the needs of the church without reservation. Therefore, every husband must also follow the example of Christ and strive to provide for his own wife, and the Lord declares that he will provide for his needs according to his glory in Christ. Needless to say, Husbands must not be afraid or anxious to take care of the needs of their wives (Philippians 4:19).

Moreover, the Bible admonishes the husband, that besides the provision and resources provided for his home and family, he is also advised to live with his wife in an understanding way, showing honor to the woman as the weaker vessel, since she is heir with you of the grace of life. You must therefore be mindful so that your prayers may not be answered (1 Peter 3:7).

It is evident that when a husband and a father provides the needs of his family, he will in turn experience the abundant benefits of acceptance and obedience to the commandments given for the head of the household; and he will not undergo lack and poverty, because he has diligently hearken to the commandments of God.

There is no gainsaying that a man that fails to provide for his household, plans to lose that that family to a better provider. Moreover, he is exposing himself to ridicule, shame, and disgrace. But the worst aspect of it is that he exposes his children begging, stealing, covetousness and lust at other children who are well provided for; and he will inadvertently turn his wife into a women of evil desires and easy virtues for the sake of providing for her children whom you have neglected.

Subsequently, you may lose your children and wife to a more honorable man and a caring husband.

Heaven has a lot in store for any man who is willing to align his will, plan, and purpose with that of God, and ready to follow obey the commandments of an excellent provider as enunciated in the Bible.

Prayer

My Lord and my father, I thank you for being the great and perfect provider. Father, in your mercy, endow me with the heart and mind of generosity to be an honorable provider for my wife and children in the mighty name of Jesus.

References

Matthew 7:1-29, Mark 8:36-37, Acts 16:31, John 3:3, Romans 6:11, 23, Romans 10:9, 1 Corinthians 13:1-13, 2 Corinthians 12:10, Galatians 2:20, Ephesians 1:6, Ephesians 5:1-33, Philippians 3:13-15, Hebrews 12:1-2, 2 Peter 3:18, James 1:2-3.

CHAPTER SIX

Be Your Family Guard Rail

*He who dwells in the shelter of the Most High will abide in the shadow of the Almighty. I will say to the L*ORD*, "My refuge and my fortress, my God, in whom I trust." For he will deliver you from the snare of the fowler and from the deadly pestilence. He will cover you with his pinions, and under his wings you will find refuge; his faithfulness is a shield and buckler. You will not fear the terror of the night, nor the arrow that flies by day. Psalm 91:1-16*

A husband of a wife and the father of the children has been given one of the most essential and crucial roles as the head of his family. This role is called the protector. I called this head of the household, the guard rail of his family. A guard rail is defined as a support that prevents people from failing off or being hit. It is also a strong fence, a barrier, against danger, to reduce the risk of an accident. Therefore, it behooves the head of the household to ensure that he provides a fortified physical barricade against infiltration to his dwelling place and his family members against harm or hurt. However, the most significant protection for your family is that of their spiritual wellbeing.

As the head of your household, you must use any means legal within your power to sanctify, fortify and preserve the lives of your family from any intrusion.

The lives of your household are anchored on your shoulder, and it is your sole responsibility, regardless of your situation, to see that nothing is missing and damaging to your home. The lives of your wife and children are sacrosanct and must not be defiled or violated.

We understand that father Abraham was concerned with the safety of his nephew, Lot, that he asked God to spare his life, and when Lot was taken away in a war with the Canaanites, Abraham deployed with his massive servants to go to war against the Canaanites to rescue Lot. Therefore, as a husband, you must never permit anything to disturb the joy and peace of your family.

The Bible is replete with the promises of the Lord concerning your family. In Isaiah 54: 13-17, the Lord says your children shall be taught by the LORD; have peace and be established in righteousness. It further declares that you will not need to be afraid, because you will not experience oppression, but the Lord will remain your refuge and your fortress.

If you take the calculated risk to defend your household, you will receive abundant honor, grace, and acceptability in the presence of God. This is an honorable task to take, and the Lord promised that he will charge his angels to provide protection and ensure that you do not dash your feet against the stone (Psalm 91:11).

Your protection for your family is not limited to physical barricade, you are also called the spiritual gatekeeper of your family. You must ensure that your wife is busy in assisting with the training, mentoring, and modeling of acceptable character traits to your children, providing the godly moral principles for the children to emulate. The children must not be allowed to socialize with the wrong friends, so that their characters are not maligned and contaminated. As a father your children must not engage in filthy activities or profess in evil communications, For the bible admonishes that bad company corrupts good character (1Corinthians 15:33).

It will be in the interest of a honorable husband and father as the shepherd, the gatekeeper of his house that will make the face of God shine on him, the hand of God supports and strengthens him, and the grace of God to perfect everything that concerns him, and for his acts to be acceptable by God.

Prayer

O Lord my father, I thank you for being a shield and refuge for me. Oh Lord, empower and strengthen me to provide a fortress and protection for my entire household as your chosen gatekeeper.

References

Deut. 31:6, Psalm 23:1-6, Psalm 32:7, Psalm 46:1, Psalm 91:1-16, Proverbs 18:10, Isaiah 41:10, Isaiah 54:17, 2 Corinthians 4:8-9, Hebrews 13:6.

CHAPTER SEVEN

Be a Firm leader in Your Home

For if someone does not know how to manage his own household, how will he care for God's church. 1 Timothy 3:5

The Bible places the leadership of the home squarely on the shoulders of the man and the husband of the home. The Bible calls him the head of the household. The Lord created him first, gave him the reins of the affairs of the Garden of the Eden, and mandated him to tend, cultivate, control, and dominate it. God also brought all the animals he created to the first man, Adam. He permitted him to give them names, and the names Adam gave them retained till today (Genesis 2:15-20).

This situation therefore presupposes that God wants Adam to take the lead in his home. It does not mean he will be a dictator, or an oppressor as the head of the household. It was for this reason that God created Eve to be his helpmeet, to provide adequate assistance to him whenever the situation calls for it. Hence, he was not alone in figuring out all the answers by himself. The same situation applies to the modern man today. He is authorized to take charge, operate from the front, handle anything that may confront his home, wife, children, and proact against suspicious situations. With his wife beside him, he can bounce his ideas and thoughts back and forth and solicit for the necessary input. However, in no sense should a man dump, or relegate his decision making on the lap of his wife and expects her to make a perfect choice in the circumstance. Her roles are defined as a helper and to procreate. Although she has the obligation to assist, suggest a series of suggestions or alternative ideas, she must not be the definitive solution provider. The onus of coming up and taking the last decision lies with the head of the household, and this must be at the focal point of his mind.

Nonetheless, many heads of the household have relinquished this herculean, yet honorable role to their capable wives, who are all too willing and assertive to take over this task. Unfortunately, when this happens, a series of concerns are generated. One of such issues is the man completely abdicating this responsibility. The wife takes over the family decisions, and by so doing, the man begins to become less relevant in the scheme of the home affairs. She rarely discusses prominent issues her husband should know about, she begins to run the affairs of the children on her own; and before long, she has eroded the significance of the headship of the man.

When the situation degenerates to this level, the man begins to lose his relevance not only to his wife but also that of his children.

The implications of this could weaken the security and stability of his home, it could make the man lose the rein of the affairs of the family, and if care is not taken, the children's training, counseling and admonishment will slide, and it may erode the significance and strength of his position as the head of the family. Any man, who knows his God, loves the Lord, and trusts in God's promises and declarations, will not hesitate to align his plan, desire, will and purpose with that of his God. If he knows this, there will be abundant grace in everything he does, he will have tons of favor from all and sundry, he will be abundantly blessed, physically, materially, and otherwise because he has totally tuned himself to the frequency and the wavelength of God's mandate.

Prayer

Oh Lord my father, you bless any man whose eyes are on you. Lord, I lift my eyes on you, asking for your direction, instruction, knowledge, and wisdom to help me run the affairs of my home successfully. Lord, let your word be the light onto my feet, and the lamp unto my path.

References

Psalm 103:17, Psalm 119:32, Proverbs 11:29, Proverbs 15:20, Acts 10:2, Romans 12:5, 9, 1 Corinthians 13:4-7, 1 Corinthians 9:24 1 Corinthians 9:25-27, Ephesians 6:4, Ephesians 5:25, Galatians 5:7, Colossians 3:19, 1 Timothy 3:4, 1 Timothy 5:8, 1 John 4:19, 1 Timothy 3:4.

CHAPTER EIGHT

Give Your Children What Matters Most

Every good gift and every perfect gift are from above, coming down from the father of lights with whom there is no variation or shadow due to change. James 1:17

It is a natural desire for a father to want to provide for his wife, but more so for his children. It is a phenomenon that is mysterious and complex to the natural mind. Nonetheless, it may be spiritually explained, because the desire and ability to give others what they need, and are affordable to release such things, stem from the concept called love. The Bible tells us that God is love, and if we are supposed to worship him, we must do so in spirit and truth. Love is an inexplicable, deep-seated emotional feeling that emanate from one person to another usually for the opposite gender, but Love is a concept that is attributable to all human entity, regardless of color, gender orientation, status, young or old, rich, or poor. On the other hand, this idea of providing for another person has been spiritually explained by the sacrifice of Jesus Christ on the Cross of Calvary.

The Bible explained that the heavenly Father, loved us so much that he wants to reconcile with us, despite our abominable sin; and the only way he can prove his love is for him to send his son to die for us for the atonement of our transgressions. Therefore, it is understood that the earthly father will also want to give his best to his family, whom he loved and cared about.

Father, one of the most beautiful things you have been endowed with, is the ability to procreate. The blessing to reproduce yourself and your wife in another human being is incredible. God is concerned both about the care and nurture of the child or children you are about to bring to life. But most important, is what sort of ways you are going to raise those children, what kind of counsel you are going to give them, what kind of gifts you are going to blessed them with, and what legacy are you preparing to leave them with?

The Bible declares that children are the heritage from the kingdom of God, the fruit of the womb is a reward. Like arrows in the hand of a warrior are the children of one's youth. Blessed is the man who fills his quiver with them! He shall not be shamed when he speaks with his enemies at the gate (Psalm 127:3). Children are unique and special that they are the inexpressible gift of God (2 Corinthians 9:15).

Christ was as enamored with children that he was indignant, when his disciples were reluctant to let them come near Jesus, and Jesus declared: "Let the children come to me; do not hinder them, for to such belongs the kingdom of God (Mark 10:14).

The beauty of the Lord is so great on children that the Lord declared in Isaiah 54:13-17, that the children will be for signs and wonders; that they shall be taught of the Lord, that the children will not be oppressed, they will not be afraid, but will be established in righteousness, and peace will be their portion. The Lord further declares that he will not allow any weapon designed, manufactured, or schemed to prosper in the lives of the children. This is the unfathomable depth of the Lord's love for your children.

Every good and loving father wants to give his children the best of education, provision of the best physical and material wellbeing, cars, exquisite lifestyle, and grandeur on many levels. There is nothing wrong with these provisions, but these gifts are temporary, perishable physical things, which are not necessarily the best things a father can provide and leave behind as a heritage for his children.

Among the best things a father should and must provide for his children, are everlasting things that are acceptable and approved by God. These are:

- **Love: Fathers,** Love is a fundamental attribute of God. In fact, God is love and he exemplified this by sending Jesus Christ to come to earth to show us, how much he loves us. Therefore, as a man of God, as a father, you must demonstrate the love, care, and concern for your children. You must tell them about the unconditional love of God for them, you must teach them what the Lord think of them and how much he loves them. Teach them also to love the creation of God and show compassion and empathy for their fellow man.

- **Christ Gospel:** You must introduce the gospel of Christ to your children. They must know what Christ sacrificed for them to have life, and what the gospel teaches them about forgiveness and redemption of their sin. Tell them about the goal of making it to heaven. Remember that this is the last mandate that Christ left behind (Matthew 28:19-20).

- **Word of God:** Fathers, it is imperative that your children read, meditate, and study the word of God. They must have the word of God in their heart and mind, so that they will not sin against God. When you expose them to the word of God, they will be able to apply it in times of stress, trouble, and trial (Psalm119:11).

- **Training:** The Lord wants you to know that one of your crucial responsibilities to your children is to train them for their usefulness in future to you as a father, and for themselves. The Bible says when you train them the right way they should go, they will not grope in darkness, they will not stumble, fumble, falter and fail. This is necessary for you (for them, and acceptable to the Lord. Proverbs 22:6).

- **Counsel:** As a father, it is incumbent on you to admonish and give wise advice to your children. You must tell and teach them to stand for the right things and abhor everything God hates, and advise them to stay on the right path of righteousness. The bible says that with abundance of counsel, you can wage a war and there will be victory (Proverbs 11:13).

- **Truth:** Head of the household, father of children, you are to teach your children to stay on the path of truth, stand on truth and tell the truth, even when everyone is on the false and lie trail. The bible says that Jesus is the way, the truth, and the life, and no one can come to our heavenly Father without him. Therefore, your children must know who Jesus Christ is and let them submit to him (John14:6).

- **Kindness and Generosity:** Fathers, as the head of your households, while you show kindness and generosity to your friends, the Bible also mandates you that you extend the same love, kindness, compassion, and generosity to your own family and your household. These attributes must also be demonstrated to outsiders. This what the spirit of the Lord calls for, and it has effects of eternal benefits.

When a father provides adequate discipline, divine and wise counsel to his child on constant and regular basis, it is evident that such child will grow in admonition of the Lord. However, the greatest gift a man can bestow his child goes beyond temporary, perishable things. A godly father must ensure that his child knows and appreciates the beauty and goodness of the Lord. He must teach him to have reverential fear of the Lord, respect his sovereignty and omnipotence. As a caring and loving father, he must endeavor to demonstrate and share the love of Christ, as the father of all fathers. He must show him the significance of Christ, and what he represents in his life, and what he means for his eternal destiny.

The Love of Christ and his word must be paramount above the legacies he shares with his child, and he must see to it that the child also love the Lord with his heart, soul, mind, and with all his strength (Deuteronomy 6:5). When he succeeds in all these areas, then he has given his son the best of all gifts. He must make him understand that a life without Christ, will eventually have a collision course with crisis, calamity, and woes. These gifts couple with the fact that he must also teach him to be humble before man and God, because the bible declares that God despises a proud and arrogant man, He must teach him to respect and treat others the way he would like to be treated, demonstrate and practice in the presence of his child the different attributes of the gifts of the spirit.

His child must learn to empathize with others in disadvantaged situations, he must be able to show kindness and generosity to others, have compassion for the poor and the needy, and have gentleness and calmness to rule his emotions and spirit. These are few of the lasting, enduring gifts and untainted legacy that a godly father must strive to impart to his child, so that his way may be prosperous and have good success, just as God commanded Joshua regarding his own children (Joshua 1:8).

Prayer

O Lord, my Father, I thank you for the lovely gifts of redemption and salvation of my soul. Lord, give me the grace and the will to train and bestow my children with knowledge, understanding and wisdom of your word, your unlimited grace, the joy of your salvation and the eternal gifts of heaven.

References

Psalm 127:3-5, Proverbs 22:6, Proverbs 22:6, Isaiah 54:13, Matthew 18:10, Mark 9:37, Mark 10:14, Ephesians 6:4, John 3:16, James 1:17, 3 John 1:4.

CHAPTER NINE

Align with God's Will, Plan, and Purpose

If I speak in the tongues of men and of angels, but have not love, I am a noisy gong or a clanging cymbal. And if I have prophetic powers, and understand all mysteries and all knowledge, and if I have all faith, so as to remove mountains, but have no love, I am nothing. If I give away all I have, and if I deliver up my body to be burned, but have no love, I gain nothing. Love is patient and kind; love does not envy or boast; it is not arrogant or rude. It does not insist on its own way; it is not irritable or resentful. 1 Corinthians 13:1-13

The blueprint to tread on the path of righteousness, have a prosperous way, lead a peaceful and calm life, and have good success is not established in intellect, good behavior, position, fame, and power. But it is deeply rooted in the manual of God, which is the Holy Bible. However, men that have tried to rule from the position of power, money, and fame, have stumbled and fell (James 1:5).

The Bible is replete with the memoirs of kings, warrior and men of substance who had tried to achieve fame and glory, but failed God and disappointed themselves.

At creation, we read that the world was void and in stark darkness, but when the Lord decreed light to appear, the entire universe as we know it today is dominated with brightness. The sun is God's light for the day and the moon for the night. All these came forth at the instance of God's pronouncement (Genesis 1:1-3). Similarly, God specifically instructed the first human, Father Adam, to cultivate, control and dominate the Garden of Eden, he had lavishly and pleasantly provided for his habitation and survival. But because of Adam's utter disobedience of God's instructions, life went haywire for him, his wife, and children (Genesis 3:17).

Adam's afterlife was a testament that no man could live a rich, abundant, and successful life without doing it God's way. No creation of God will refuse and fail to partner with God, and expects to thrive, flourish, and live in peace. Subsequently, we read about the diligence of Abraham who trusted God at his word, though he faltered due to his wife's conviction, God saw Abraham as a man with trust and believe in his word, and God accounted him to be a righteous man. This presupposes that no one can made a good, abundant life without working and tail gating the path and instructions of God.

Father, it will be in your interest and those of your household, if you will be committed to align with the laid down doctrines, principles, and precepts of God. If you will love what God loves and hate with passion what God abhors.

Being the head of the family, if you will work, plan, and obey the will and words of God, you will experience God's hand of elevation, promotion, and protection. If you as the father of the house will allow the purpose of God to be your guidelines to work with, and carry along your household, ensuring that you are in tandem with God's unshakeable commandments, then you and your family will be extravagantly rewarded. When you adhere and follow through, you will not only succeed, thrive, and flourish, but you will also operate at a sacred spiritual dimension with God, where you can fellowship with him, hear his directions distinctly for you and your household. Here he will show and tell you his sacred secrets and mysteries which he does with those that abide in him and his words. Your experience as a man and a father will be different from so many ordinary people who are not in consonance with God (Jeremiah 33:3).

This is how far from God is ready and willing to go with anyone that will dare to submit, align, and cooperate with him. Consequently, it will be a disastrous end, if you remain obstinate and unyielding to the rules and laws of God. If truth is to be affirmed, there will be serious crisis of calamity and woes. If you fail to synchronize yourself and your desires with that of God, especially when he has made his plan and purpose known to you. It will certainly not augur well.

There can be no success, peace, joy, protection or safety, and victory. Without Christ in your life, in your home, all will be nothing but crisis. So, I implore you to work with God in all his ramifications and enjoy all the divine benefits he has reserved for you and your household.

Prayer

Oh Lord, my father, I thank you for your divine way, will, plan, and purpose for my life and my family. I bless you that there is peace, protection and victory in your words and your ways. My God, I ask that you shine your light of illumination into my heart that I will have the will and strength to partner with your plan and purpose, in Jesus' name.

References

Genesis 1:1-3, 1 Samuel 15:22, Joshua 1:8, Isaiah 1:19, Jeremiah 29:11, Jeremiah 33:3, Matthew 7:21, Luke 6:46, John 14:15, John 14:23, Acts 1:8, Acts 19:1-41, Romans 6:16, 1 Corinthians 13:1-13, Philippians 2:8, Hebrews 13:17, James 1:22.

CHAPTER TEN

Man: A Pillar of Purpose in Church, Community, and the World

I have written at length the myriads of responsibility God have deliberately placed upon the man's shoulder as the divine chosen gatekeeper. These responsibilities are herculean in nature. A man may decide to embrace it as an undeserved and gracious honor upon himself and run with these responsibilities, seeking help from God, and taking due advantage of all the available tools of assistance and vehemently hanging on to the hem of God's providence, power, grace and mercy to carry him through the treacherous decadence world we all live in. If he finds God's deliberate mandate as an honor he does not deserve or earned, he will appreciate it, and he will grab this incredible, awesome, and inexplicable honor from the Lord. By so doing, it will lead him in the prosperous way he should go and will amount to achieving good success. Meaning that he follows the pathway of righteous and good stewardship.

Perhaps, this man thinks, acts, behaves, and follows his own understanding and perception of life and his responsibilities, thinking he knows the how and ways to navigate the course of his life without following the laid down prescription of prosperity and success originally laid by God, it may not augur well as he has purposed or presumed. There will be crisis, chaos, and confusion along the way. This is the reason why God has called man His representative on earth to mirror what He is doing in heaven. This is the only way his endeavor can be successful. Anything outside of God's wisdom, knowledge, understanding and guidance, there will be an avalanche of crisis and disaster (Proverbs 3:5-6).

A man lacking discernment and conviction of the immeasurable power of God, will consider his position as the divine gatekeeper of his family as a control and a burden from the Lord, rather than a favor, grace, and blessing. That man will not appreciate this deliberate blessing and favor from the Lord.

Having indicated God's mandate for man in his family. The Lord does not limit his gatekeeping responsibilities to his household alone. Definitely, the family is his core priority. A man that cannot take care of his family is worse than an unbeliever who does not submit to God. His family is his fundamental responsibility.

However, his mandate transcends beyond his money. The man God has divinely chosen, is expected to have a significant impact in his church where he worships. He must strive to project a good Christian individual, assist the leaders in the church with progressive ideas, his time when needed, and money if he is meant to support any church agenda that will benefit the congregation. He also has the responsibility to confer with the leadership of the church if he finds any untoward behavior in them or among the congregational members. As a father in his own home, he should be prepared to nurture, train, and aid within his capability to other children in the church if he observes any untoward, act, attitude, or behavior among the youth and others in the church.

The man that God has chosen as His gatekeeper on earth should not limit his influence on the home and church alone. His community needs his engagement, his skills and talent, and his exemplary behavior and attitude for others to emulate. His co-workers must be able to see a responsible, loving fatherly, a humble Christian in his utterances and demeanor, and a leader willing to take care and risks for the enlightenment and elevation of his organization. He does not have to be the chief executive officer of the organization before he proffers excellent ideas, suggests alternative solutions to protracted and complex issues. This and many more responsibilities are in his roles as God's gracious gatekeeper.

Men have been seen to attend to the issue of diplomacy among nations. They are the ones that have the prowess to process and declare wars, and they are the ones that are known as combatant soldiers among other tasks. They did not choose these functions by dint of their finite wisdom and intelligence. God deliberately built their physical attributes and components to be capable to withstand hard and heavy load, intense, stressful, and complex work. Prophetically, it translates that there is a demand for men to step up to their function as the divine gatekeeper. Just as God calls his own people a chosen generation and a royal priesthood, and a peculiar people, which are also the responsibility of every man (1 Peter 2: 9).

Furthermore, men are duly charged with the duty and the task to ensure the safety, security, and the wellbeing of his nation. His nation must be defended at all costs, while his skills, time, and talent must be harnessed to make the nation run like a well-oiled machine for its citizens. We noticed that the Lord indicate that man is supposed to be a lively stone, and built up as a spiritual house, a holy priesthood, to offer up spiritual sacrifices, acceptable to God by Christ Jesus. This is God's heartfelt and thoughtfulness toward man spiritual gatekeeping. (1Peter: 2:5). Furthermore, men are the ones assigned to staff the gates of the tabernacle and control the access to it (1 Chronicles 9:23). As gatekeepers, man and the rest of humankind are first to guard the gates of our lives, the ears, eyes, mouth, mind night dreams at all times (Proverbs 4:23). Just as he is mandated to be in charge of the spiritual gates of his family, churches, communities and nation through intercession to ensure that enemies and Satan do not have access, and that God's divine purpose as well as his peace are not defiled, and contaminated, but must thrive with the family and the rest of the other life components (Proverbs 14:19).

As spiritual watchguard of their homes, churches, community, nation, and the world at large, the man is expected to prevent surprise attacks by warning the people in the community or in the nation of any suspicious or impending danger. As men of discerning spirit, they are also to watch out for signs of forthcoming blessings in the homes and community and provide the avenues and open the gates to allow them in. Being the spiritual security guard over his family and his church and community, he is supposed to discern God's plans, detect enemy strategies, provide protection, and ensure there is an offensive response to catapult such enemies (Ezekiel 3:17). All these herculean responsibilities should be taken seriously, because God will eventually demand for man's account of his stewardship (Ezekiel 33:4-6).

In view of the decadence pervading our decadent world, God required men expected to maintain the prosperity, success and joy of families, marriages, secure money, and treasures in the house of God, and the stability of the home, city, and nation (1 Chronicles 9:26). When men are painstaking alert, careful and focused on these arduous responsibilities, homes will be joyful and saved, families will thrive, community will prosper, and the nation will stabilize, flourish, and be at peace.

CHAPTER ELEVEN

The ABCs of Salvation

For by grace, you have been saved through faith. And this is not your own doing; it is the gift of God, not a result of works, so that no one may boast. Ephesians 2:8-9

The concept of salvation is not a mystery. It is a concept that is backed by the Almighty God himself. The idea of salvation came about because of all the abominations we have committed against our creator and our Father, Salvation is an answer to our separation from God because of our transgressions and iniquities.

Consequently, due to the unconditional love of God, He said his only begotten Son, to come to the world to come and show us the way, to come and pay the debt of sin, death and hell that you and I cannot pay, and to go on the cross of Calvary to die for our sins, and reconcile us with our heavenly Father. This is the essence of Salvation (John 3:16).

This is the fundamental basis for salvation. But what does it take to have salvation.? To be admitted into the kingdom of God, you will and must first repent of your sin and transgressions, submit to Christ. You must accept Christ, believe that he is the Son of the heavenly Father, and confess that he is your personal Lord and savior. Then you will have the power to be called the Son of God, be in God's kingdom, and have your name written in the book of the lamb, the book of life. The Bible says that if you believe in your heart and confess with your mouth that Christ is Lord to the glory of His Father, then you will be saved. The following steps are the way to salvation.

- **A:** This stands for **ACCEPTANCE**. Here you must accept that you are a sinner, and you have come short of the glory of God. It signifies that it is because of your sin that you become separated from God. Then what do you do next? (Romans 3:23).

- **B:** This stands for **BELIEVE**. You must be that Jesus Christ is the Begotten Son of the heavenly Father. You must believe that Jesus came in flesh, that he went on the cross of Calvary, that he died, that his blood was the atonement for our sins, and prevent us from going into death and hell. The Bible says that if you believe in Jesus, out of your belly will flow rivers of living water (John7:38).

- **C:** This stands for **CONFESS**. You must confess, proclaim, and spread his love and his lordship over you, share his love for you, and share his message of truth, way, and life. When you do this, you are in the God's kingdom. You have the power to be called the son/daughter of the Highest God. You have become BORN AGAIN, Christian. Hallelujah!

Beloved, when you have done this, it is time for you to join a bible-based, Christ-focused, living church, and begin to serve God and have a sincere relationship and fellowship with God through our Lord Jesus Christ. Amen!

Prayer

Oh Lord, my Father, I thank you for your ultimate divine sacrifice, and unconditional love. Thank you, Lord, for saving me from the sin, death, and hell, and saving me. I bless you that you have written my name in the book of the Lamb and I have eternal life.

References

Psalm 37:39, Psalm 62:1, Matthew 7:21, John 3:16, John 14:6, John 15:1-27, Acts 4:12, Acts 16:30-33, Romans 10:9, Ephesians 2:8-9, Galatians 2:21, Titus 3:5.

www.ingramcontent.com/pod-product-compliance
Lightning Source LLC
LaVergne TN
LVHW041555070526
838199LV00046B/1971